I0168604

Learning to Live in Colour

A Poetic, Journey,

Through

Neurodiversity,

Unspoken Truths, and

the Light Beyond

Fauve Thorpe

William Cornelius Harris Publishing
In collaboration
With
London Poetry Books

ISBN 978-1-911232-65-0
Copyright © Fauve Thorpe 2026
All rights reserved

14 Fairlawn 159 Kingsway Hove

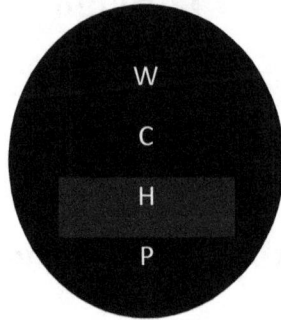

W
C
H
P

London Poetry Books

Dedication

For my sister, Keeley
your absence shaped these words,
and your memory colours every page.

For my dad, my granddad, and my nan
your love and your loss live on within these poems.
For my dear friend George, and for his mum, Ann
your story holds a place of remembrance here.

For all my family and friends who are no longer here
too many to name, but never forgotten.

For Jeannie, my closest friend,
and for my family and friends who carried me when I could
not carry myself.

For the neurodivergent community
may you find in these poems the reflection, recognition,
and hope that so often felt out of reach.

For Lost Souls Poetry and for Hannah,
thank you for giving me space, courage, and opportunity
to speak aloud what once was silence.

And even for those who hurt me,
who taught me the contours of manipulation and pain:
your shadows shaped this work too,
and in that shaping, you helped me find my colours.

Contents

Learning to Live in Colour

A Poetic, Journey,
Through
Neurodiversity,
Unspoken Truths, and
the Light Beyond

Fauve Thorpe

Shadows

The Invisible War

The invisible war is the war I most fear
the war in my mind that rings in my ear.

It's a war I witness every day
a war in my mind that's stuck on replay.

My brain lives in fight, flight, or freeze.
I'm always on high alert
always on the edge
like I could fall or be hurt.

A dark shadow gives me a piercing stare
I turn around it's gone, no longer there.

The biggest battle is the one I fight
with myself
with my own mental health.

A battle with your brain
leaves wounds and pain,
But no one sees because this battle
wears the mask of invisibility.

It isn't until you're screaming
crying
self-harming
that the battle becomes alarming.

If you're fighting an invisible war
I see you
I hear you
I ask you not to ignore.

Turn down the voices that tell you not to care.
Because peace can be made
if you choose to be brave
try not to let the war make you too afraid.

The Glass in My Mind

Why does it seem easier to break
than to put yourself back together?

Sometimes I feel broken
beyond repair.

Am I going to stay this way forever?

Fragile as glass,
I topple,
smash,
pieces scattered into my past.

Shards lodge deep in my brain
it's the smaller ones
that cause the most pain.

I feel like my mind is bleeding,
but no one can see.

The reason for the pain
is simply
being me.

Over time, the glass wears down,
becoming grains of sand,
burying my thoughts
deep within the land.

I long to break free,
but the shards cut me down.

I'm lost...
and it feels like
I can never be found.

I go
to where
the sea meets the sand,
hoping to understand.

The sea washes the glass away,
cleansing my soul,
my body,
my mind,
if only for a day.

And maybe
that's how
I'll find a way
to put myself
back together
I will find my way.

The Glass in My Mind.

The Box of Pain

We all have our own box of pain.

My box doesn't care if there's sunshine or rain.

My box doesn't care that I like to pretend it's not there.

Sometimes I feel I can contain all the pain within the box.

I convince myself I'm the master of all its locks.

But then, without warning, the locks all break open,
and the pain rushes out, and a rage is awoken.

A rage I can no longer contain,
because I tried to lock a box of pain
inside my brain.

I wish I'd never started to lock my pain away;
I guess I thought I could face it another day.

But that's the thing about the box:
even when it's locked,
if we don't let the pain out,
it can't ever heal.

And if the pain can't heal how can we ever be real?

Now I'm trying not to lock my pain in a box anymore.

I'm learning to ease it and find what I can use it for.

Because sometimes,
there's power in the pain we feel
and when we begin to process it,
we start to heal.

Sometimes, we need to unlock our box of pain,
if only for a while,
because as we begin to heal,
we might find a smile.

No feeling lasts forever
and unlocking the box is a vital endeavour.

Afraid of Food

"You are afraid of food?"
I hear her say.
I simply answer, "Okay."

Being thin is desired, admired
a narrative passed from you to me,
but one I can never agree.

We chase the elusive thigh gap,
fashion and media selling us
a thousand products to make us thin

Never warning
of the state of mind
it leaves us in.

Next time you say,
"Your thighs are too fat,"
remember: being thin ain't all that.

It steals your love of food,
your joy, your mood.

Don't become afraid of cake,
or forget how to celebrate.
Now, I celebrate recovery.
This journey,
My journey of self-discovery.

Welcome to the Shitty Committee

Welcome to the shitty committee.
What is the shitty committee?
I hear you ask.

It's that voice inside your brain,
the one that drives you insane
the one that tells you you're no good,
because it is misunderstood.

It tells you that you can never
achieve your dreams.

But as hard as it seems,
you must not listen to that voice in your head.

You must try to put that voice to bed.

Dreams weren't given to us for no reason,
just like the changing of the season.

The shitty committee keeps you
in your comfort zone.

The shitty committee will bitch and moan.
But in our comfort zones we never grow,
and we never get to show
all the talents that we share.

So now I declare:
don't listen to your shitty committee.

Because at the end of the day,
the committee's just a little bit shitty.

In Therapy

In therapy,
we talk about the fact
that I'm a work in progress.

But I must confess
I'm still trying to process
the trauma from my past.

I find the feeling of peace
at Everlast,
but still,
guilt,
anger,
and shame
whirl around in my brain.

And all the time,
I question
if I am insane.

The pain of the past
never seemed to heal,
and then we wonder
why we end up
mentally ill.

We were never taught
the skills we needed
to process the emotions
we keep inside.

We spend our lives
trying to hide
the pain and the trauma
we live with every day
always wishing
we could make it go away.

But wishing
never got anyone far.

It's just a fairy tale
that you can wish
upon a star.

That's why I use poetry
to lay it bare.

I use the power of words
to share.

But we can't let the trauma
of the past
define us.

We should let it
unite us
to talk
about trauma,
to heal,
to regain
the strength
to stay strong,
and carry on.

The Unspoken Words

It's the unspoken words
between moments
that hold our fears
when you're trying to
catch your breath
but can't,
because you're
fighting back tears.

Suddenly,
there's no air.
My legs are
shaking so much,
I swear
it feels like I've been
struggling to breathe
for so long.

This moment seems
like it will
never end,
and this pain feels
like it will
never be gone.

My vision is starting
to become hazy,
and I'm desperately
trying
to catch my breath.

I call out,
but I can't
it feels like
I'm going crazy.

Frantically searching
for air,
I realize it's just
not there.

In this moment
of panic,
I can't remember
why
I started feeling
so manic.

The more I panic,
the harder it becomes
to breathe.

All I want is for
this pain
to be relieved.

Eventually,
I begin to
catch
my breath,
feeling
grateful
because I
thought
this was my
moment of death.

Different Fires

It Took Me 32 Years

It took me thirty-two years to realize
that I wasn't actually an awful person,
that I wasn't truly bad.

When I reflect on this now,
it does, in fact,
make me truly sad.

I always struggled to make friends.
No matter how hard I tried,
I could never seem to make amends.

If I did something wrong,
I didn't understand what I had done
and that wasn't something
I could just overcome.

I spent my life thinking:
There must be something wrong with me.
Why does nothing ever come easily?

People always seemed cruel and unkind
and for some reason,
that was what stuck in my mind.

The bad thoughts went round in my head,
stuck on repeat.

I couldn't escape them.

I couldn't retreat.

So, there was a battle in my mind,
and I was becoming blind,
because I could not see
that these bad thoughts
we're destroying me.

He insulted me
in front of all our friends.

But I told myself:
I'm a bad person,
so, it's my fault
I must make amends.

He screamed in my face
in the middle of the street,
and I thought:

Because I'm bad,
I should just retreat.

I'm such a bad person, I thought
maybe I can try to be a little sweeter.

It's my fault he became
a wife-beater.

I could never escape these thoughts
that I was rotten to my core.

I wished there were a way
to simply shut the door.

But those bad thoughts
had always been there
lurking in the back of my mind,
trying to give me a scare.

After my dad and sister passed away,
the bad thoughts consumed me
and that wasn't okay.

They told me:

"You're such a bad person
that's why everyone close to you
just dies."

And I believed it.

I didn't realize
those thoughts were just lies.

I genuinely believed I was bad
for so long.

But now I understand:
those bad thoughts were wrong.

I've recently learned
that many of my struggles
are because I am autistic
not because I'm a bad person.

My thoughts
were just
a bit unrealistic.

Autism Awareness Month

Do you know what?

I hate Autism Awareness Month.

Because no one can decide what it should be called.

You can't call it Autism Awareness Month
because you can be aware and still do nothing.

You can't call it Autism Acceptance Month
because you can accept it and still do nothing.

Guess what?

You can call it Autism Understanding Month,
and still do nothing.

So, what is the point?

The emphasis on language is far too great.

At the end of the day, it doesn't matter what you call it
it will still be a debate.

You don't understand what it's like to be autistic,
and it's as simple as that.

I'm not sure if any campaign is ever going to change that.

So, you can talk away about what it should and shouldn't be called,
but this language debate has nobody fooled.

It's a distraction from the real problem at hand.
It doesn't matter what it's called if you don't take a stand.

Campaigning means nothing if real adjustments can't be made
otherwise, there is no point to this endless charade.

Call it what you want, but actually try to understand.

And try to change
and please, just stop telling us
that autistic people are the ones to blame.

Perception of Rejection

Rejection Sensitivity Dysphoria (RSD)
a word that was once unbeknown to me,
until I learned it,
and could finally see
why I felt
all of these emotions
so negatively.

Rejection feels like pain
I cannot describe
it's a whole new level,
a whole different vibe.

It's not just sensitivity to rejection,
it's also sensitivity
to the perception
the perception
of being rejected.

Your mind can't handle it.
It can't be deflected.
So, you become a people-pleaser,
just to feel protected.

But people-pleasing
never protected anyone
it only stopped me
from saying the truth,

from getting things done.
Now I'm trying to undo
all the tears
and all the years
I spent
trying to please everyone.

It feels like such a heavy weight
a ton of pressure
I can't quite measure.

Because my fear of rejection
is just too great.
What I wouldn't do
to obliterate
obliterate that fear,
obliterate the people-pleasing
I used for protection...

Because I don't know
if I can handle
yet another rejection.
But the one thing I've realized
it's all just perception.

So, I will try
to look at rejection
in a different way.
It won't be easy
it might take a month,
a year,

or just a day.
But every time
I choose to look at rejection
with kinder eyes,
I start to realize:

RSD is part of my brain
and maybe,
I can just ease that pain.

Maybe I can handle rejection
a little bit better
next time,
and realize

that I just need
to draw the line...

and not let
my RSD
define me.

L and R

I want to get L and R
tattooed on my hands.
They tell me I'm mad.
I just say,
"Okay."

They list the tricks
to learn left from right
as if I've never heard them before.
Explaining it again
feels like a chore.

But they don't understand.
I have tried.
My brain doesn't work that way.
That is why
I wanted it tattooed
on my hand.

I wish it were as simple
as they say.
I wish there was
a magic pill
to make it go away.

Living in a dyslexic mind
is complicated.

That's why
I chose the tattoo
to show the world
I'm not afraid
of who I am.

They think they understand
what dyslexia is like.
I want to tell them
take a fucking hike.
Dyslexic minds
are powerful,
creative,
innovative.

Just because
we struggle with "simple" things
doesn't mean
our minds can't fly
can't take you
on a journey
with words we share.
And so,
I declare:
I love
my beautiful dyslexic mind.
Because my dyslexic mind
is a gift
not a flaw.

Being a Dyslexic Poet

Being a dyslexic poet
can feel a little problematic
and no, I'm not saying that
just to be dramatic.

I feel embarrassed
when I stumble over the words
I'm trying to say.
Sometimes, I just wish
my dyslexia would go away.

Because people often assume
you're unintelligent.
They think you're dumb.
And that perception?
It's a heavy one to overcome.

My words don't always come out
as I planned,
yet still
I get up on stage,
I take the mic stand.

Even after all this time
I still get tongue-tied
and terrified...
but I manage to stand here somehow.

My poetry?
It's never perfect.

But by God
the fear,
the stumbles,
the shaking hands,
the misread lines
they're worth it.

Because the more I speak,
the more I share,
the more I dare
to take up space
the more I feel proud
to be standing in this place.

I know I'll never remember
my poems by heart.
But that doesn't make them
any less
of a piece of art.

Sometimes, all you need
is the courage
and the chance
to start.

The Deficit Narrative

If you haven't heard of the deficit narrative
around neurodiversity,
let me take you on a journey.

It began over a century ago,
and it just goes to show
how negative ideas tend to stick
for some reason,
we can't seem to get away from it.

We hear claims like
"No empathy"
or "disordered cognition."
But honestly
that's just a fucked-up definition.

My brain isn't disordered.
It's just a different way of being,
and I find that perspective
incredibly freeing.

If all our brains were exactly the same,
wouldn't that be insane?
Imagine a world without diverse ways of thinking

How would we create?
How would we explore, or engage in debate?

How could we truly learn from one another
if we spent all our time
comparing ourselves to each other?
And yet, the deficit narrative persists
that's why these harmful ideas
continue to exist.

So, I ask you
challenge what you think you know
about neurodiversity.
Do you understand what it's like
to face a lifetime of adversity?

The deficit narrative distorts the truth,
leaves an image that's hard to reframe,
while neurodivergent individuals
are so often unfairly blamed.

I will continue to challenge this harmful view,
and I urge you to reflect
on what you think is true.

Because out of all the lies
this narrative dares to sell...
the "no empathy" lie?
That's the one that hurts
more than hell.

You Call This a Trend

When people tell me
that being autistic and ADHD
is now just a trend
or worse,
they say it's just pretended.

So, what's so fashionable
about being so exhausted
that you can't even speak?

You can't even move
not a muscle,
you feel so weak.

You feel stuck
in thick, oozing black tar.
You want to walk across a room
it feels so far.

I spent my whole life
feeling so inadequate,
and feeling so lazy
my life felt like a constant battle,
and I was just labelled crazy.

I always felt like I was battling my emotions,
drowning in a never-ending river.

I was constantly trying to control them
but then they would make me quiver.
And the quivering would lead
to emotions desperately trying to escape,
to do anything
to try and break

Break down my whole body...
and then it would begin to shake.
All of a sudden everything stopped.
My whole body just dropped
dropped wherever I was,
simply because...

My emotions don't have any restraint.
And that's a terrifying thing to contemplate.

Sometimes I would scream
a scream that would split your ears.
And then there would just be
floods and floods of tears.

I would be sobbing
like somebody murdered me
and that is what a meltdown is like,
to me, you see.

And then you have to live
with the constant fear
if anyone witnessed your meltdown,
they'd call it bad behaviour.

They would lock you up
while pretending to be your saviour.
They would lock you up
and put you in a mental institution
mistaking your meltdown
for a mental delusion.

So can someone please explain to me
how living with autism and ADHD
is now considered super fun...
and trendy?

Tell me
is that really what you call trendy?

Oliver

I'd never heard Oliver McGowan's name.
Now I'll never forget it
his story filled me with shame.

He was sectioned
just for being autistic.
It's terrifying, yes,
and feels so unrealistic.
They gave him antipsychotic medication,
as if that's the answer
in this nation.

"We'll drug the distress,
that's how we care.
No need to ask
what pain is there.
Just pump him full
and call it best.
Tick the box,
forget the rest."

Unfortunately, Oliver had
a terrible reaction
to that medication.
So, they placed him
under constant observation.

No privacy. No space.
Just walls and eyes.
He was watched around the clock
but no one heard his cries.
Every hour. Every day.
No silence. No space.
Just rules to obey.

He grew more distressed
flinching, folding in.
No soft lights. No quiet.
Nowhere felt safe for him.
The staff spoke down,
slow and loud,
like he was a child.
"What's the fuss?"
they muttered,
as he spiralled.

So, they gave him the meds
again.
Though his notes said don't.
And he said no.
No one listened.
They just signed off,
and let it go.

The doctors said
they didn't know
that giving those meds
would cause such a blow.

But Oliver's death
was the price he paid
for warnings ignored
and wishes betrayed.

They saw his fear,
but missed the sign.
His brain was wired
by design.
His distress was not
some deep condition
but autism,
not a new admission.

The way autistic people
are treated in these places
must stop.
How many more lives
need to drop?

How long must we carry this cost
before you admit
that you're the ones lost?

Hidden Empowerment

I see so many things about empowering the neurodivergent community,
yet for me, I can't seem to see.

The empowerment they talk about is the importance of our voices
but suddenly, if we don't align with precisely what you want,
you take away our choices.

I really don't see this empowerment.
Where is it? It's hidden somewhere I just can't seem to find.

All I keep seeing is injustice, playing in my mind.
We're still fighting to be heard,
to be seen, to be understood
constantly met with: "you should," "you would," and "you could."
Parents fighting for their children just to access education,

while robbing the neurodivergent of disability support
is somehow saving the nation.

God forbid we actually help people when they're in need
but I guess that's too much to ask
in a world ruled by corporate greed.

There are so many wonderful people trying to help,
and so many people who truly care.

Such a shame they're stuck in a system
that's broken beyond repair.
It's left everyone feeling nothing but despair.

People have tried to take my voice from me,
but they will never succeed
because I will never bow down to corporate greed.

I will keep fighting until I've got nothing left.
I will keep fighting until my very last breath.

Because my voice will be seen,
and it will be heard
and I will never, ever be deterred.

The Invisible Mask

I wonder which version of myself
I will share today
who I will present to you,
who you will see.
I contemplate
whether anyone even knows
the real me.

Because the invisible mask I wear
has become part of my armor.
It's how I became a people pleaser,
and somewhat of a charmer.

When people say my mask
makes me fake or fabricate,
to me that opinion
seems outdated.

My mask was the only protection
I had to survive.
It wasn't like I plotted,
or planned,
or contrived.

There was a time I believed
my mask was woven
into the fabric of my being.
Because I was such a people pleaser,

I never disagreed.
I didn't even understand
that having personal boundaries
mattered
because I had none,
and the few I did
were shattered.

At times this world
was so heartless
and that was when
my world was filled
with nothing but darkness.

There were so many people
claiming they were compassionate,
understanding,
sympathetic
but those were the people
who tore me down
and called me
pathetic.

So, I moulded myself
into someone
people might admire,
or appreciate.
I just wanted
to find someone
who could relate
relate to the feeling

of being worthless,
of being hollow.

At the time,
I was always hoping
for a better tomorrow.
But tomorrow never came.
I carried my guilt
and shame.

One day,
I decided to break free
from that invisible mask.
I tore it off,
smashed it up
but even that
was a harrowing task.

And I'm left
with one question to ask:

Does anyone even know me
behind the invisible mask?

Bruises You Can't See

Invisible Scars

When you say you were abused,
everyone expects you to be battered and bruised
but there's a different type of abuse,
one of the mind.
One that is silent.
One that is cruel.
One that's unseen... yet unbearably unkind.

It leaves invisible scars nobody else can see.
It leaves you questioning,
Will anyone ever believe me?
We're always taught
that violence is wrong.
But we're never taught
that emotional abuse
can be just as strong.

This type of pain doesn't show up in X-rays.
It shows up in flashbacks, in panic attacks,
in the way you flinch when someone raises their voice
even if they mean no harm.

Maybe it's time we uncovered the truth.
The truth about what abuse really looks like.
And maybe just maybe
we can put that truth to good use.

Teach the next generation
that all abuse is wrong
not just the kind you see on skin,
so, they won't repeat the pain
I've carried within.

The Manipulation Playbook

The Manipulation Playbook
Let's take a closer look.
I swear these narcissistic individuals out there
must have a playbook hidden somewhere.

It's like they share a secret code
I've seen the same behaviours
play out so many times.
Sometimes, you just have to read between the lines
and realize they're all playing the same game.

The aim is to manipulate you,
to screw with your brain,
to make you believe you are insane.

They'll make you believe it's all your fault
these are lessons that the playbook taught.

They gaslight you until you feel like you're on fire,
because to them,
you are nothing but another possession to acquire.

Narcissists will try to break you.
But what they don't realize
is the human spirit being strong.
They will never have a place
where they truly belong.

So, wherever your playbook may be,
just don't forget:
I'm on to you.
And you can't manipulate me.

In the Leagues of Men

Within the leagues of men,
they try to rate you from one to ten,
then throw a backhanded compliment
every now and then.

Am I supposed to be flattered
that you rated me?
Am I supposed to feel complimented
that you don't hate me?
Your ego is so big
it needs a number,
and I just sit there and wonder.

You say you don't understand
why women don't like you,
and you pretend
you don't have a clue.
You tell me we're in the same league
but mate,
we're not even the same breed.

I was taught to be kind
and compassionate toward everyone
and yes, that includes you.
But don't mistake my kindness
as proof that I automatically fancy you.

Don't tell me your feelings for me
are my fault.
Because you're nothing but a misogynist bastard,
and you just got caught.

So yes, you can stand there
and rate me from one to ten
but I don't give a shit.
And I don't take shit
from little, tiny, misogynist men.

The Tide of Truth

I remember when you were like the sea,
holding me afloat so delicately.
Warm, calm,
with an irrefutable charm.

But the sea's surface can deceive the eye.
There's something intoxicating about it,
almost leaves you feeling high.
Beneath the water's calm disguise
was the mirage, the mirror
you created so effortlessly.

Then the waves grew heavy,
too strong.
The mirror cracked.
The blue turned black.
Out of the abyss,
I saw the true you
a snake in disguise,
a life built on lies.

Your venom infected my brain.
For a time,
I believed I was insane.
I tried to escape
the prison you built,
but your poison
always seemed to win.

54

Until the day
you pushed my boundary too far.
And finally,
I saw who you really are.
I fought for shore,
fought harder than ever before.

And though your poison lingered,
it taught me this:
I must be kind
kinder to myself.
That's how I learned
to reclaim my mental health.

So don't let the poison of the past
destroy who you are now.
If you still carry venom inside,
you will get through it
somehow.

What You Can't Take from Me

There was a time you took so many things from me.
Back then, I was broken into a hundred pieces,
and I just couldn't see.

But there were things you could never take.
You couldn't take my voice.
Now I speak and you've got no choice
but to listen to what I have to say.
And all the things you failed to take away
still stand strong today.

You couldn't take my kindness, my laughter, my humour.
So, you tried to drag me down by starting a rumour.
But I don't care if the rumours were believed.
I let go of how I'm perceived.

Why should I care about opinions
from people who weren't even there?

They only met one of your personalities.
I had the misfortune of meeting them all.
So many masks, so many personalities
you might as well be an avatar.

God help anyone else trying to figure you out.
My advice to them: run, without a shadow of a doubt.
The truth is you tried to destroy me
with what you thought you took.

But none of it truly mattered
those parts of my life won't even get a second look.

So, cheers to you. Congratulations you failed.
And cheers to me,
because I am the one who prevailed.
And I always will.

Bring It On

People are starting to wake up,
people are onto you.
They can finally see your manipulating ways
but I'm not sure what to do.

Because you're still playing this game,
still trying to manipulate,
still trying to silence us,
to shut down the debate.
But fractures are appearing in your team,
cracks in your façade,
fault lines in your dream.

I feel lost,
stuck,
sad
but also angry,
and kind of mad.
Because I know I'm not crazy.
I see what you're doing,
clear as day.
But I don't know what to do
should I just walk away?

I can't let a manipulator win,
but I'm tired of being used as a pawn
in this endless game I'm trapped in.
So maybe I'll keep my cards close,
try my best,
find a way out of this mess.

Because truth is worth the cost,
even if gaslighting twists me
and makes me feel lost.
I know I'm not crazy.
I know this battle is worth fighting.

So, bring it on.
I won't back down.
I will stay strong.
So come on, bitch
bring it on.

The Game Ends Here

Sometimes I wonder
how a person could be so cruel, so unkind.
It's like you have no soul
or maybe a soul made of steel.
I would have definitely been dead
if looks could kill.

That's the thing with you:
it's always written all over your face.
You try to hide it,
but I can't keep up with you
you're just all over the place.
One minute you seem kind,
seem to care;
the next, you've flipped a switch,
and there's a new personality there.

It is mentally exhausting
to try to keep up with you
and your hundreds of personalities
the pain and anguish I feel
because of the attempts you make
to change so many realities.
But the reality is
this mental exhaustion
has taken its toll.

In the end,
things went spinning out of control.
I had to deal with
all the darkness that came flooding back
the darkness that destroyed so many things,
the darkness I thought had set me back.
But this time
there was the tiniest bit of light
of hope,
and a tiny bit of aspiration.

Because I realized
that in order to destroy me,
you'd have to destroy
a whole fucking nation.
Because I've been broken
more times
than anyone can quite conceive but I still believe.
That in spite of the torturous pain
I have gone through,
I'm a better person
because of you.

The pain you caused
taught me a lesson
I needed to learn
and I hope one day
you will get your turn.

Learn to grow,
to change,
to hopefully become
a better version of the person you are now.
Although personally,
I don't see it
but I still wish it, somehow.

So good luck to you.
So, thank you.
And now I can finally say:
the game ends here,
and I'm glad it's over, my dear.

www.ingramcontent.com/pod-product-compliance
Lightning Source LLC
Chambersburg PA
CBHW071358090426
42738CB00012B/3153